The Teenagers' and
Young Adults'
GUIDE
to the WORLD of WORK

Cheryl Campbell

Kingston, Jamaica

Published by Cheryl Campbell
Kingston, Jamaica
cherylhopebooks@gmail.com

ISBN: 978-1-7375431-1-4

COVER DESIGN: Michael Robinson
PAGE DESIGN: Krystal Cameron Designs

NATIONAL LIBRARY OF JAMAICA
Cataloguing-in-Publication Data

Name: Campbell, Cheryl, author.
Title: The teenagers' and young adults' guide to the world of
    work : preparing our future leaders to take flight. / Cheryl
    Campbell.
Description: Kingston : Cheryl Campbell , 2023. | Includes
    bibliographical references.
Identifiers: ISBN 9781737543114 (pbk).
Subjects: LCSH: School-to-work transition. | Career education. |
    Youth employment.
Classification: DDC 370.113 -- dc23.

CONTENTS

INSPIRATION

☾

"I see you working with young people, teenagers and young adults, and the impact on them is going to be so great that even their parents are gonna want to come and say, 'I need to get a piece too' because what they're gonna see in their children and young adults will be so impactful!"

Prophetess Marsha Hill
Restoration World Outreach Ministries International (RWOMI)
(Prophetic word received on May 21, 2021)

DEDICATION

☾

I dedicate this book to my teenage son, Johnathan Clement Ewers.

Johnathan, at the time of writing this book, you are 17 years old and recently graduated high school, with your focus set on pursuing your first degree. I hope you will find some value in this book and that it will form a major part of your intentional preparation to chart the exciting journey of your personal and professional life.

I wish you much success in your career, the corporate world and as a young entrepreneur. In fact, I can confidently declare and decree that if you apply the principles and nuggets shared in this book, your own success will be so unprecedented that it will astound, even you!

The world is yours for the taking, so take flight, my wonderful son as you are a natural leader!

ENDORSEMENTS

☾

We are not surprised that Cheryl has released her second book in less than six months! There is a great deal of knowledge and experience displayed on the pages, and that, coupled with all she shares as a result of her own spiritual growth will bring significant change to the readers!

Teenagers and Young Adults, as you open the pages, do so with great anticipation, and an expectation that you are about to get excellent, thorough preparation for the world of work.

This book has the potential to increase your confidence and self-esteem as you get ready to enter the corporate world!

Here you go!

Apostle Dr. Steve & Pastor Dr. Michelle Lyston
Restoration World Outreach Ministry International

The Teenagers' and Young Adults' Guide to the World of Work is an excellent resource tool for all teenagers and young adults, as they prepare to embark on a new adventure in the world of work.

This is timely information which so many persons will benefit from, even for some of us who are already on the adventure and are still learning to navigate the different twists and turns of life. The information is fulsome and gives all the tools needed to embrace the corporate world and be successful in navigating.

From preparing for that first interview to negotiating that first salary, this guide answers all the questions. Work ethics, professionalism, conversation, attire and navigating personality types are just a few of the areas that are covered, and which I found to be so necessary and useful, especially at this time.

Although I have been in the work environment for many years, this guide has been a great resource for my children and I.

I believe every teenager and young adult should own a copy of this book. It will definitely equip them and give them the needed edge to compete and win in the game of life and master the challenges of the corporate world.

A must have for every home library!

Karren Goulbourne Emmanuel, Educator

"The Teenagers' and Young Adults' Guide to the World of Work" is the book I wish I had when I was merely thinking about "adulting".

Navigating the work world is work in and of itself but you don't have to feel alone because Cheryl Campbell is here to the rescue.

Skillfully addressing the pertinent topics of preparing you for work, the author shares this information in a way that is easy to grasp. Not only that, but she also does more than tell you what to do; she shows you how to do it by including sample application letters, resumes, etc., to guide you along the process.

Heneka Watkis-Porter, The Entrepreneurial You

ACKNOWLEDGEMENT

☾

I was blessed to have had an amazing mentor and coach when I was a teenager. This was in the person of my third form, mathematics teacher, Mrs. Christena Ralph.

She was the most influential mentor and coach in my life, then, and helped to bring order, comfort, spiritual direction, guidance and reassurance to my, sometimes, turbulent teenage years. I received much sage advice and counsel from her about the world of work, as I later navigated the vicissitudes of the corporate life.

I wish to honour Mrs. Ralph with this book, and I am excited to pass on much of the knowledge and wisdom gleaned from the corporate world to expectant teenagers and young adults who are ready to take their own flight!

Bon voyage teens and young adults!

FOREWORD

☾

Cheryl has done it again!

Determined not to overlook the teenagers and young adults, after releasing her first book, *Processed on the Threshing Floor of Life*, Cheryl has now published her second book, *The Teenagers' and Young Adults' Guide to the World of Work.*

What a timely book!

What an instructive book!

An essential and critical must-have book for today's Millennials, Generation Zs and future generations, yet unlabeled or undefined.

This book also provides mentors with a great mentoring tool to coach this generation into success!!!

Congratulations Cheryl!

I am so proud of you, and I am already looking forward to your third book!

Apostle Courtney McLean, Founder & Senior Pastor
Worship & Faith International Fellowship, Jamaica

INTRODUCTION – A PERSONAL NOTE

☾

The Teenagers' and Young Adults' Guide to the World of Work with the subtitle, **Preparing our Future Leaders to Take Flight**, is an excellent and comprehensive guide to prepare teenagers and young adults for the corporate world. It covers topics across a continuum from preparing one's mindset for the work environment to getting and keeping the job plus all that comes in between to guarantee the teens' and young adults' corporate, professional and personal success.

Never has there been a book with such depth to comprehensively prepare our teens and young adults for the corporate world, as they seek to leave home, college or university and embrace the exciting world of work. This book serves as their second "bible" or handbook with invaluable secrets to steadily climb the corporate ladder, become an influencer and create global impact.

PART ONE

THE EARLY DAYS
OF MY CAREER

CHAPTER

1

THE ANTICIPATION

I can feel it again!!

I am 14 years' old, and I am trying on my elder sister's heels and her dress that I could not even fit into. But the thrill of the thought engaged my imagination to make it work.

I looked at myself in the mirror and walked back and forth, strutting my stuff, as it were, visualising that I was actually working as an adult, earning my own money and living on my own. I felt that rush again! I felt that thrill of excitement! Nothing could compare to the anticipation I felt as adrenalin filled my mind, body and soul!

I cannot wait, I think. How soon is the time going to come? How much longer do I have to wait to leave home, to earn my own money, to shop for what I want, the food I want to eat, the clothes I want to wear and my personal necessities, so I would not have to ask my parents for money? How long?

Ohhhh! Independence coupled with freedom was beckoning me with open arms! My desire was very strong!

Here I was salivating at the number of bottles of Horlicks that I would buy; not to mention the sweet condensed milk and delicious milo. I thought of the frosted corn flakes or plain corn flakes with the granulated sugar sprinkled on top of the milk so when I took a mouthful, I could crunch it and feel the sugar grain grinding in my mouth! Hhhmmm! With my own money, I could buy any amount I wanted, and no parent could tell me I could not!

Cornflakes was a rare treat at home while I was growing up and what a precious treat it was especially when it came directly from "the great America"! In my child's mind then, anything that came from America was, truly, very good!

The corned beef was also very good; I think I remember it tasting better than the local Grace corned beef with rice! I also remember going to my mentor for the weekend, and she would prepare corned beef with sweet peas and serve it with cabbage mixed with sweet corn; both with rice was simply to die for! So delicious!

All I knew was that I wanted to work and quickly!

Indeed! I wanted to "come of age" very quickly so that I could be catapulted into the exciting world of work! This would ensure my independence from my parents and grant me some exciting financial possibilities!

CHAPTER
2

IT HAPPENS!

Finally, I got my wish!

He came for me! And quite unexpectedly!

It happened one Saturday evening while I was spending the weekend with my mentor. My uncle found me in the country and said he had come to take me to the big city of Kingston, as he had been able to arrange a summer holiday job for me. I was to start the following Monday!

I could not believe my good luck! I could not believe my ears! I could not believe my eyes! I was beyond excitement!

I was in the first year of college by then and about 15 plus years of age. I would turn 16 two months later.

CHAPTER
3

MOVING TO THE BIG CITY

I journeyed to Kingston to live with an aunt in the big city of Kingston. She lived with her daughter and I was to board with her while I worked.

It was so intimidating to me! The buses! The blaring horns on Eastwood Park Road in Kingston!

I had to get familiar with the bus system. I had to take a bus from Meadowbrook Estate where I lived to Half-Way-Tree and then from Half-Way-Tree to Downtown Kingston to go to my first summer job. Then, I had to find my way home in the evenings.

I remember passing my stops accidentally a few times. I was so nervous and did not want to come off at the wrong stop. But, it was all part of the major adjustment of living in the city!

Country girl come to Town!

CHAPTER

4

MY FIRST SUMMER JOB

I never liked my first summer job. But I had no choice. After all, I had got my dream to leave home just to start working and earning my own money! It was with the National Import-Export Bank of Jamaica, a subsidiary of Jamaica's central bank. The cost of lunch at the Bank of Jamaica where we would eat was only J$1.00, as it was a major subsidy and benefit to employees.

I think at the time I was paid about J$120.00 per week. Yes, believe it or not! It was in the late 1980s. Only J$120.00 per week based on my recollection. I remember having to pay my aunt about $25.00 out of that towards my boarding; the rest was mine to save and buy my clothes and shoes for work.

Finally! I was so proud to earn my first salary and do my first corporate and personal shopping.

CHAPTER
5

MY FIRST TEMPORARY JOB

Towards the end of the summer, I was offered a temporary job at the Bank of Jamaica in its Exchange Control Department. This was at a time when exchange control regulations were the norm in Jamaica.

I was a secretary in that department and worked there for two and a half years, as I patiently waited for management to lift the freeze on recruitment and appoint me to permanent staff. After that time and when I saw no hope of permanent engagement, I had no choice but to leave to take up a permanent job with another company.

My time at the bank was interesting, and I even got the opportunity to act as a Senior Secretary in the Exchange Control Department. This was such a boost to my self-esteem and my intrinsic motivation. I started to learn just a little about office politics, office relationships, people, staff policies, training and development, et cetera.

The world of work had started to open up to me with all its positive and negative facets. I was certainly learning along the journey in the world of work.

CHAPTER

6

MY FIRST PERMANENT JOB

I just knew I had made a mistake! My first corporate mistake!

Standing there, almost non-plussed, at the entrance to the new company, I could tell that I should not have left the bank for this construction company. My heart sank! Why did I leave? I wish I could run back to the bank. And quickly! How I wish I could return that resignation letter! Anyway, I proceeded like a self-assured, confident young woman and made my way towards the entrance door of my first permanent job.

It was a fairly good experience on the journey in the world of work.

CHAPTER

7

MY EARLY WORKPLACE LESSONS

1. **Do Not be a Walk-over.** Not because someone is older than you or has more seniority than you means that you should accept anything, everything and be spoken to in a condescending or disrespectful manner. Resist subtly but respectfully and assert yourself diplomatically while still treading carefully as the "new kid on the block". Once your colleagues, supervisors and managers see this, they will respect you from early in your onboarding and will be careful not to disrespect you.

   In this regard, the scripture, 1 Timothy 4:12 says:

   > *Don't let anyone look down on you because you are young, but set an example for the believers in speech, in conduct, in love, in faith and in purity (NIV).*

2. **Have a professional opinion on company matters and be prepared to share that opinion when asked.** Do not give the impression of a waffler or that you are an indecisive person. This increases with experience and confidence, and you will be more respected as a professional. A few years later in my job experience, I always remembered sitting in a board of directors meeting and

looking at one of the directors who could never take a definitive position on anything. As I looked at him, I secretly lost respect, as that told me a lot about him. No one could ever tell where he stood on issues, and that is not a good position to take. Either you are in your corporate position to add value and make a meaningful contribution or you are not.

3. **Be selective about your choice of company or who you befriend**. You are truly known by the company you keep and, believe it or not, that also, goes for the workplace or corporate. For instance, if some of your colleagues are already known to be disruptive, too quick to challenge every company policy, confrontational and inclined to gossip, avoid joining their cliques; otherwise, you will be labelled with them, and this may hurt your future promotional opportunities.

4. **Constantly review the workplace policies and the content of the Employee Handbook** so you can be assured of always adhering to company policies, especially the company's code of conduct. In so doing, you will avoid infractions that may blemish your professional reputation and character, as these are sure to be placed on your personnel file.

5. **Familiarise yourself with the employment/labour laws in your country**. If you do not, you could subject yourself to being taken advantage of by unscrupulous employers who play on your ignorance.

CHAPTER 8

CAREER DAY/WEEK

Many schools, colleges and universities traditionally host Career Days for fourth and fifth-form students annually. I certainly benefitted from Career Day events during my high school and college years.

Hindsight is 20/20 but I think more should be done to prepare teens psychologically, mentally and emotionally instead of just functionally. The focus seemed then to be always on explaining the career jobs that could be considered as career choices and what those jobs entailed. Nevertheless, I encourage you to make use of all the Career Day/Week activities and Job Fair opportunities to constantly improve your awareness and knowledge of the career options that obtain. This exposure will greatly inform your career choice.

PART TWO

PREPARING FOR THE CORPORATE ENVIRONMENT

CHAPTER 9

PREPARING YOUR MIND

The scripture in Romans 12:2 says, "And be not conformed to this world but be ye transformed by the renewing of your mind that you may prove what is that good and acceptable and perfect will of God." It also states in Proverbs 23:7, "For as he thinketh in his heart, so is he."

Remember that your thoughts create your mindset and drive your emotions. Your emotions drive your behavours. Your behavours will inform your actions and your habits. Your habits will determine your lifestyle and decision-making choices – always!

Your thoughts will also guide your interpersonal relationships with others and determine your speech, image and degree of self-confidence and self-awareness.

☾ May I suggest that you do a "**mind audit**" to determine your unpleasant or negative thoughts that result in negative feelings and consequently, negative experiences.

I have learnt to be so in tune with my thoughts that if I am alone and, suddenly, I get uptight (which I usually feel in my shoulders), I then ask myself the question, "What thoughts immediately preceded the physiological reaction in my temperament or feelings? Having retraced my thought pattern in that very moment, I can usually identify the cause or catalyst of that negative feeling and, sometimes, resulting action.

❨ Once you identify the negative thoughts, assess how they hurt you in the past and contributed to some of the negative experiences or relationships in your life.

❨ Also, assess how they continue to impact your present life and outcomes.

❨ Eliminate them by intentionally telling your conscious and subconscious mind that you "are not that thing"; that you are, in fact, the opposite of that thought. Use self-talk such as, "I am more than a conqueror; I am the head and not the tail; I am above and not below; I am emotionally intelligent and my emotions are subject to my control – they do not control me." You can get even more specific by saying and repeatedly affirming the opposite of what you feel and what your conscious mind tells you, but you must convince yourself of this so your subconscious can be just as convinced. Only then, will you be victorious in this effort and see the results you wish.

❨ Constantly reinforce those positive affirmations and empowerment statements **daily** until they are accepted by your subconscious, and you automatically become the affirmation you practiced.

❨ Why daily? It is said that a negative habit must be replaced by a positive one which is consistently practiced over twenty-one days or more for it to be sustained and become a part of your natural behaviour.

Confidence

Once you take care of your mind and win the battle mentally, confidence is automatic. This trait is extremely important! Even when you do not feel confident, you must act with confidence. This is imperative as the lack of confidence affects your thoughts, your posture, your temperament, your personality, your relationship with others, your performance on the job and many other areas. Your lack of confidence is also felt by others.

With over 30 years' corporate experience and about 20 years in various businesses that I operated, I cannot underscore this point adequately. In fact, I considered it important to write a separate topic about it.

When you start out in your first job, you will experience the following range of emotions:

- ❀ Uncertainty
- ❀ Doubt in your ability, capacity and skillset; after all, you have had no experience whatsoever unless you were blessed to have got a few summer job opportunities previously.
- ❀ Inadequacy
- ❀ Lack of confidence
- ❀ Intimidation
- ❀ A sense of being overwhelmed
- ❀ Excitement
- ❀ Anticipation
- ❀ Freedom

Of all the above, if you can renew your mind to have **unshakeable self-confidence**, that will take you a far way. Even knowing that you have no experience, your self-confidence will send a very powerful message to your subconscious mind and cause you to automatically act with confidence, speak with confidence, walk with confidence, work with confidence, relate and interact with confidence.

CHAPTER 10

PREPARING YOUR CONVERSATION

1. The following tips will assist you in being a great conversationalist:

2. Be well read and read widely on a range of subjects to be informed, as this has a major impact on your ability to converse generally, intelligently and knowledgeably. In so doing, make use of professional journals, major newspapers, professional articles and jargons, world news, et cetera, to be informed.

3. Travel when you can for the exposure and watch the Travel Channel to learn about countries and their cultures.

4. Have an excellent command of the English Language, as this language is universal; this cannot be overemphasized. As a Human Resources Consultant and practitioner with many years' experience, I have observed in corporate that it is the person who is an excellent and effective communicator (written and oral) who advances the corporate ladder quickly.

5. Develop powerful phrases to use in your communication that cause you to be conspicuous.

6. Join professional associations, especially in your chosen career; for example, if you are a Human Resources practitioner, become a member of the international body that represents Human Resource professionals, i.e., the Society of Human Resource Management (SHRM).

CHAPTER

11

PREPARING YOUR ATTIRE

1. "First-dress impressions" definitely last; yes, not just "first impressions" last!

2. You cannot go wrong with the classic, traditional office attire, i.e. the classic jacket in navy blue, grey and black, so invest in at least one of each.

3. Know the professional colours and wear them; they are grey, navy blue and black.

4. If your budget is small and it most likely will be for your first few months in your first job, ensure that you have some basic pieces such as a black or navy-blue blazer for both males and females and a black and navy-blue pants and skirts or shift dresses for females.

Females

1. Females should, at a minimum, have a black blazer and a navy blue blazer which can be worn over a shift dress or inner camisole with matching skirt.

2. Invest in some camisoles and start off with varying colours such as navy blue, white, beige, grey, red and pink. Then rotate them.

3. Black and navy-blue pumps are also ideal, especially patent shoes which stand out.

Males

1. Invest in a black and a navy-blue blazer at a minimum.
2. For the more formal organisations that require the wearing of ties, ensure you have some appropriate ties but remember the colours baby blue, pink, black, white, yellow and grey.

CHAPTER

12

PREPARING YOUR RESUME

Sure File-13 Triggers

The following practices will ensure that your resume hits "File-13" which means recruiters discard it. Do avoid them so a recruiter can stop and not just look at your resume but invite you to attend an interview.

❮ An unprofessional email address/account and especially one which has sexual undertones, e.g.:
  ✿ sexygirldonna@hotmail.com
  ✿ hotguydon@yahoo.com

❮ Do ensure that you take out a new professional account that you can use on your resumes.

❮ Gaps in employment dates/tenure

❮ Omission of past experiences

❮ English errors, e.g. spelling, grammar, poor diction, punctuation

❮ Poor presentation

- (Too lengthy resumes
- (Too small a font thereby making your resume illegible
- (Repetitive duties and responsibilities – verbosity!
- (Frequency of job moves (as this depicts instability and lack of loyalty)

Sections of a Resume

Let us look at the sections of a resume:

Contact Details/Your Letterhead

- (Name – ensure the correct name is used; if you did a deed poll in the past, adhere to the new name resulting from the deed poll. You may also mention this in the interview.
- (Title – if you have a title, ensure it is used, e.g. Junior (Jnr), Senior (Snr) and so on.
- (Telephone numbers – ensure all numbers provided (home, work or business and mobile) are working numbers.
- (Email addresses – ensure your email is current and constantly checked for spam entries or full inboxes
- (Home address (vs job location) – it is good to provide both a residential and a mailing address; however, there is nothing wrong with providing a mailing address if the specific residential address may lead to recruitment bias based on a geographic location. Just be honest in your response if asked by the interviewer about your residential address, as failure to provide accurate information could lead to your termination if the truth comes out.

Career Objective

This should genuinely be aligned with the expectations and requirements of the job being applied for.

Achievements

This is excellent and strongly recommended especially if the job being applied for is one that is heavily result oriented, such as a Sales Manager or Sales Director role, a Marketing Director or Marketing Manager role, a Business Development Manager role, etc. Why? Because your employer will be looking to ascertain the following actual results from the various related positions held in your career history:

(Revenues raised

(Sales targets set and achieved

(Dollar value of savings accrued to previous employers for various projects

(Receivables managed including liquidation of bad debt portfolio, if any

(Size of capital and operating budgets managed

Career Span/Professional History

1. Always start with your current employment and work backwards to your earliest career stint.

2. Ensure that you present the place of employment, location and job title of each position held, followed by a brief description (no more than four bullet points) of the major job functions executed.

3. Ensure that no gaps are present and that if any exist, they are accounted for with an explanation, e.g. *2005-2006 – I took a hiatus from the corporate world to pursue the dream of a world tour or to pursue the birth of my child.*

4. Another approach is to represent the position with the direct relevance to the role first after listing your current role rather than starting with #1 above.

5. Yet another approach is to do a Career Summary of your experience relevant to the job being applied for and/or in accordance with the specifications of the job advertisement.

Qualifications

1. If an academic course of study is being pursued, include the time started and that it is ongoing at the time of your resume preparation; also indicate the possible end date.

2. If there are incomplete courses, indicate the reason briefly e.g. incomplete due to financial constraints or simply omit all incomplete courses. You can opt to provide the related information and explanation during the interview as the opportunity presents.

References

It is acceptable to simply note "Available upon request".

Affixing a Photograph

There is no rule of thumb to include or not to include a photograph of yourself. If you do, it should be a professional photograph and not a casual or sexually suggestive one. I personally do not think it is necessary.

Always bring a physical copy or two of your resume, printed on professional resume paper (ivory, white or light grey) when attending an interview, along with your academic certifications. Additionally, always have an updated copy of your resume for presentation at any time, if requested.

CHAPTER 13

PREPARING FOR YOUR FIRST INTERVIEW

PURPOSE OF A JOB INTERVIEW

☾ To get to know the job applicant

☾ To match the face to the resume

☾ To verify information supplied in the resume

☾ To verify the qualifications/credentials

☾ To simulate the job environment and observe the candidate's response

☾ Most importantly, to observe the behaviour and attitude of the applicant generally and during behavioural assessments

BEFORE THE INTERVIEW:

☾ Prepare, prepare, prepare

How?

- ☾ Download relevant interview questions and answers
- ☾ Role play these questions with a professional or expert interviewer
- ☾ Research the company and, if possible, the head of the department you expect to work in using sources, such as social media, networks, personal contacts, et cetera.
- ☾ Ensure extra copies of your resumes are printed and take these to the interview with your credentials.
- ☾ Decide on your professional attire (*See appendix for suggested business attire images*)
- ☾ Where possible, visit the company to see the exact location, so you can make adequate transportation arrangements and be punctual.

WAITING IN THE FOYER:

My Experience - I deliberately walked through the foyer so I could discreetly glance at a prospective Human Resources Manager who was waiting to be interviewed. I was just the CEO's Executive Assistant, but I knew something about professionalism. I could not believe when I saw her applying her lipstick, sitting right there in the public foyer! That told me everything I needed to know about her! I knew she was the wrong choice. It turned out that she was!

Your Preferred Experience - So, you are now in the foyer waiting to be seen. You are seated fifteen minutes before your scheduled interview time. This gives you adequate time to relax, gather your thoughts and observe the culture of the organisation, as you watch visitors and staff come in and out of the reception area. You watch the interaction to gauge the camaraderie or lack thereof amongst employees.

Time spent in the foyer can be invaluable in telling you about the culture of the organisation. Never underestimate these ten to fifteen golden minutes.

While you wait, be careful not to engage in the following:

☾ Speaking on your cellular phone even if it is a business call. Your focus should be totally on your pending interview.

☾ Engaging in conversations with the receptionist or other candidates if you know them.

☾ Using the foyer to freshen up your makeup, adjust your clothing, or relax, e.g. remove your shoes, apply your lipstick, comb your hair, etc.

DURING THE INTERVIEW:

☾ Be pleasant

☾ Maintain eye contact at all times – not doing so suggests that you are a shifty person and are hiding something

☾ Maintain a high energy level   low energy is pathetic and is a great turn off for many recruiters

☾ Be positive

☾ Be convincing

☾ Be assertive

☾ Speak positively and respectfully about your current and previous employers

☾ Give examples of the value that you intend to bring to the organisation without embellishments

☾ Be real – authenticity can be sensed

☾ Be honest and forthcoming with information

☾ Think quickly on your feet; however, if you need more thinking time, to stall, you may repeat the interviewer's question slowly. Alternately, you may say, "Please give me a moment to think about it." This is quite in order especially when you have been answering the questions readily, fluently and intelligently.

☾ Answer questions directly and adequately without talking excessively and circuitously

● Show that you are prepared and did your research on the company and the role for which you applied

● Ask intelligent questions not found in your research, e.g.

❀ The financial stability of the company, if a private company

❀ The company's five-year strategic plan

❀ Promotional opportunities

❀ The type of culture

❀ The leadership style of the management

❀ The turnover rate of staff

❀ The "any other duties" found on most job descriptions

INTERVIEW DON'Ts

● Don't ask about compensation and benefits in your first interview or even your second interview until it is first introduced by the interviewer.

● Don't dress inappropriately e.g. wearing of sleeveless attire, jeans or denim even if with a jacket, wearing inappropriate wigs and/or brightly dyed hair colour.

● Don't avoid answering questions. If uncertain, ask the interviewer to kindly repeat the question

● Don't be circuitous with your answers; instead, be direct

● Don't think while speaking

● Don't speak while the interviewer is speaking

● Don't sit without first being invited to sit

● Don't act nervous (displayed by tapping the desk with your pen, wringing your hands, tapping the floor with your shoes, shaking your body or constantly changing positions, over gesticulating, etc.)

● Don't speak in patois (if you are Jamaican) or a local dialect from your country of nationality, no matter how comfortable you feel with the interviewer.

INTERVIEW MUST DO'S

❲ Do maintain eye contact at all times.

❲ Do answer questions truthfully, directly and fully.

❲ Do be authentic.

❲ Do ask intelligent and impressive questions about the company and the role (*see some sample interview questions and answers in the Appendix*).

❲ Do smile – this reduces nervousness.

❲ Do request your interviewer's business card. If out of cards, request and note your interviewer's details (i.e., name, title, telephone number and email address).

❲ Do leave your business card as well. Teenagers and young adults, it is a great idea to design your own business cards and put a mailing address thereon. You do not have to wait until you get the "big position" or the "big title". Your card could read:

> John Brown, BSc
> Future Entrepreneur
> Telephone: (876) 895-1113
> Email: futureentrepreneurJB@gmail.com
> Mailing address: P.O. Box 2922, Kingston, Jamaica

POST-INTERVIEW ACTIONS

❲ **Send a thank-you letter within one day of the interview**. This letter serves the purposes of reiterating your strengths and fit for the position, your interest in the job and your availability to start working immediately or within a set time. It also helps to be the clincher in the company's decision to select you as the new hire for the role.

❲ Feel free to **follow up with the interviewer** if you do not get a response within one week or two of sending your thank-you letter. Many are not cognizant that this can be done. Well, who wants the job? You or the recruiter? So, go for it!

CHAPTER
14

MANAGING UNSUCCESSFUL INTERVIEWS

So, the answer is 'no'. You get that proverbial letter that reads like this:

We refer to your recent interview on January 5, 20…, for the position of …….. Regrettably, you were not selected for the role. However, we will retain your application for future reference should a similar role arise.

What do you do?

☾ Firstly, do not take it to heart.

☾ Do not take it personal.

☾ Do not think you are not good enough. You could be of greater value to another company that requires your uniqueness and competencies.

☾ Be grateful that at least the company communicated its decision to you. Some frequently do not exercise that courtesy.

❨ Call to find out where you went wrong - if you went wrong at all! This is because the feedback could be invaluable for use in your next interview. Many applicants or interviewees do not even know that they can do this! Yes, you certainly can! Be different and use the information received, as constructive feedback to make the necessary adjustments.

❨ Guard your self-confidence and self-esteem.

❨ Guard your mind set and resist giving into emotions of disappointment and discouragement. Other opportunities will arise and when one door closes, another will open in due time.

❨ If you are a believer in Christ and you know you followed all the rules and principles of interviewing, be reminded of the Romans 8:28 scripture that states *"all things work together for good to them that love God, to those who are the called according to His purpose."*

❨ Volunteer with companies until you secure viable employment or the employment that you specifically wish. You just never know if the company you volunteer with may make room for you at some point during your volunteerism especially when you take it very seriously and impress them with your performance and professionalism.

CHAPTER 15

NEGOTIATING YOUR FIRST COMPENSATION PACKAGE

When negotiating your salary, do not consider only the basic salary aspect of your fixed compensation, as that is usually taxable unless you live in a jurisdiction that is free of income tax, such as the Cayman Islands.

You will also need to find out the timeliness and frequency of future salary adjustments, otherwise you could be locked into the salary that you negotiated for at least a year or two unless, of course, you get a promotion to break the old salary cycle. For this reason, you need to consider the following list of possible benefits and allowances offered by companies and ascertain if the company that is interviewing you offers them. This can be priceless and even more valuable than just the base salary you will be earning:

- ☾ Remote work and compressed work week which usually falls under a Flexible Work Arrangements Policy
- ☾ Paid time off outside of the standard vacation and sick leave offered

(Travel benefits

(Transportation assistance

(Motor vehicle upkeep allowance

(Petrol assistance

(Elder care

(Day-care benefits

(Volunteer days

(Hiring and retention bonuses

(Learning, growth and development opportunities

(Career counselling

(Promotional and succession-planning opportunities

(Retirement packages

(Health and group life insurance plans

(Long-term sick leave

(Disability benefits

(Relocation assistance

(Hardship allowance

(Staff Loan Benefits

(Education Assistance

(Uniforms or uniform allowance

(Payment of professional fees for professional associations of which you are a member

(Overtime benefits and rates and if your position is overtime exempt

Other Key Considerations before you Sign on the Dotted Line

In addition to the above:-

a) Know the entry-level salaries and allowances attached to your position in all sectors. You have a responsibility to know this before any job interview, as only then will you know if you are being offered sub-market rates of pay for the position for which you have interviewed. This will also ensure that you can negotiate from a position of power, knowledge and confidence.

b) Still bear in mind that you have little or no experience and will, therefore, be at a disadvantage in contrast to other experienced applicants; therefore, be realistic with your salary request.

c) As much as possible, get inside sources to give you an accurate insight and description of the culture of the organisation and, very importantly, the management style and temperament of your direct supervisor and his/her manager. Why is this important? Because numerous studies during the past few years have shown that the number one reason for employees leaving companies is the quality of their relationship with their direct supervisor or manager.

One such study was a 2020 survey which was conducted by Career Addict in the United States of America. It found that 79% of the 1,000 respondents said they would consider bad leadership as a factor in deciding whether to quit their jobs. Of this number, 43% shared that they would return to their previous jobs or roles if their former bosses were replaced.

Workstars.com also shared that "A poll of over one million workers in the US by Gallup found that leaving a bad manager was the number one reason why workers quit, with 75% of those who left voluntarily doing so because of their boss and not the job itself. The relationship with a direct line manager is critical to several employee success factors including productivity, morale and engagement. But a breakdown of that relationship, for whatever reason, can lead to mistrust, anxiety and job dissatisfaction."

MANAGEMENT STYLES TO CONSIDER

Since we are on this topic, below are some management styles to consider:

- **Autocratic** – the "my-way or the highway" approach of management which manages by giving orders and directions, leaving no room for staff's input and creativity. If you do not meet them, you could be disciplined and falsely accused of not being a team player.

- **Democratic** – encourages all-inclusiveness in decision-making generally with the freedom to express one's ideas and make suggestions.

- **Laisse faire** – the style that gives almost total autonomy to employees and the opposite of a micro-manager. Employees can take their own decisions, are allowed to take risks and let their creative juices flow freely.

- **Visionary** – motivational and inspirational leaders who are primarily concerned with the "big picture" and the growth of the organisation. This style is one that leaves the daily operating activities to the team and focuses on the strategic growth and direction of the organisation.

- **Coaching** - the style of management that is highly collaborative and is focussed on the employee's growth and development. The style that takes time to bring others up to the level of excellence that others enjoy especially when deficiencies are identified and the leader knows that a little coaching and mentoring can make all the difference to that employee's success. You can only benefit from this style if you truly wish to be coached and mentored.

- **Pace-setting** – the style of management that has very high expectations and expects the same standards of subordinates; usually, the one with this style is the first to arrive at the office and the last to leave. He or she prioritises results, deadlines and quality and takes "leading by example" seriously and literally.

If you cannot measure up to this person's standards, you will experience some difficulty working with such a manager or supervisor.

❨ **Servant** – this style of management is focused on serving the welfare of the employee and is concerned about interpersonal relations in the workplace whilst maintaining a harmonious environment at all times.

I will leave you to do your analysis of which ones you think you can work most comfortably with based on your personality, work style and temperament, and which ones you think will optimise your productivity and constantly inspire you to do a great job:

As you develop in your job and glean additional experience, once you become a supervisor or manager, you will realise that you can vary these styles according to the team that you will lead, the dynamics of that team and other organisational and cultural factors.

CHAPTER
16

YOUR EMPLOYMENT CONTRACT AND JOB DESCRIPTION

Having successfully negotiated your compensation package, you should be given your employment contract along with your job description **prior** to starting the job.

Depending on the organisation that employs you, your employment contract may include the following clauses, which should be read carefully, understood and questioned where there are grey areas:

- ☾ Name of the Role or Position
- ☾ Hours of Work
- ☾ Address/location of work especially if the company has several locations
- ☾ Human Resource documentation required for your onboarding
- ☾ Restrictions or Conflict of Interest (this speaks to your ability to engage in other jobs outside of your work with the organisation)
- ☾ Remuneration including base salary and allowances
- ☾ Probationary Period

- Benefits such as medical, group life, vacation and sick leave
- Performance Evaluation
- Evaluation and Assessment
- Severability
- Intellectual Property
- Termination of employment
- Force Majeure

A job description typically includes the following:

- The title of the role
- Who the incumbent (you) reports to
- Whom the incumbent supervises, if anyone (especially if it is a supervisory role)
- The knowledge, skills and abilities (KSAs) required for the job
- The core function/job summary of the role
- The specific job responsibilities and duties
- Special requirements associated with the role

Red Flags – watch for the inclusion of any unrelated duties and responsibilities, as you do not want to be held accountable for irrelevant job functions or tasks that are not commensurate with your expertise or knowledge as well as what you agreed to upon accepting the job.

PART THREE

YOU ACED THE JOB!

NOW WHAT?

CHAPTER 17

CONGRATULATIONS!

So, you landed your first job! Wow!

Congratulations! You did it!

This is time to celebrate as it is your first major achievement on your journey to the world of work! All the job search activities, preparations, the numerous office interviews and visits have actually paid off and here you are!

This is the time to advise family and friends and celebrate by going to the movies, dinner or doing your favourite past time.

Simply, reward yourself because you deserve the personal recognition that only you can give to yourself!

CHAPTER 18

YOUR FIRST THREE TO SIX MONTHS ON THE JOB

It is critical that having got the job, you do the following:

During the Probationary Period

Recognise that the first ninety (90) days (or six months in some jurisdictions) form your probationary period. This means that you will be keenly observed by your employer who will be using this time, inter alia, to:

a) Assess if the company had made the right decision in hiring you

b) Determine the extent of your knowledge, skills and abilities displayed thus far and if they measure up to your resume and what you shared as your strengths during the interview

c) Determine how trainable you are

d) Determine your attitude to correction

e) Assess your interpersonal skills

f) Assess your emotional intelligence

g) Assess your soft skills generally

If, at no other time, you must use this period to:

a) disprove any wrong or negative impressions that may have been formed of you by your supervisor or manager

b) Show the mettle that you are made of

c) Show your knowledge, skills and abilities to do the job competently, accurately, effectively and efficiently

d) Show that you are a keen listener and a quick learner

e) Show that you have the ability to comply with all company policies including being on time, all the time, and being present each day

f) Show that you are emotionally mature and intelligent

g) Exemplify your soft skills

Why is the probationary period so critical?

Because it determines whether you will keep the job at the end of the ninety-day or six-month period or be separated from the company. Alternately, your probation may be extended for another 90 days, six months or part thereof.

Many young adults or young professionals, especially during their first job, do not know this. Because of their ignorance, they bring the wrong attitude into the workplace and work space, which causes them to lose the job during or at the end of the first 90 days.

After waiting so long to get a job, this is the last thing you wish to happen. It will only result in a blight on your employment record, which is terrible to happen so early in your career. Others who are aware of this display the best behaviour and produce at their optimum during the probationary period but slacken off once it ends or once they are confirmed.

Major mistake!

Always remember that the probationary period is the period when you "impress the socks off" your employers with your expertise, your ability to think critically, your impressive work ethics and your excellent work attitude. However, your sustained performance thereafter will ensure your longevity, retention and upward mobility in the company.

The Employee Handbook and Human Resource Policy Manual

This handbook and/or policy manual must become your immediate and early point of reference. Usually, it is a comprehensive manual of all the company's policies and generally covers the following areas:

- ☾ Your Employment
- ☾ The Company's Expectation of You
- ☾ What you can Expect from the Company
- ☾ Code of Conduct and Ethics
- ☾ Compensation and Benefits
- ☾ Leave and Attendance
- ☾ Employee Development
- ☾ Company Discipline
- ☾ Occupational Health & Safety (OHS)
- ☾ Administrative Policies

It is particularly important that you know the following policies intimately from early in your onboarding:

- ☾ Dress Code – which outlines the company's philosophy on how it wishes its employees to be represented to the marketplace while advertising its brand.
- ☾ Disciplinary Code – which outlines the infractions that can be committed by employees and the penalties for doing so.
- ☾ Disciplinary Policy – which outlines how the company administers the disciplinary process once an infraction occurs
- ☾ Grievance Policy – which outlines the procedure to manage grievances

Being intimately knowledgeable of the policies contained therein will guide your conduct and keep you informed about the benefits that you can access and how to qualify for them.

A Few Must-do's in Your First 90 Days

- **Listen keenly** to your colleague, supervisor, or manager to whom you will report and who will be delivering your on-the-job training (OJT).

- **Take excellent notes** during your OJT.

- **Avoid distractions** such as your personal cellular phone which must be on silent or off until your bathroom or lunch breaks when you can check your messages and emails.

- **Get acquainted with the unwritten practices and policies.** This is critical as not every policy, guideline or benefit/privileges will be written or included in the Employee Handbook and/or Policy Manual!

- **Get to know the personality and temperament of your direct supervisor and indirect supervisor or manager** (*See chapter on Navigating Personality Types*). It is important that you know both as in the absence of your direct supervisor or manager, you may have to report directly to your indirect supervisor or manager who happens to be the boss of your direct supervisor or manager.

- **Get to know the personalities and temperaments of your immediate colleagues in your department or unit** *(See chapter on Navigating Personality Types)*. This is important, as you will know how to relate to them. Some professionals underestimate the importance of this point and feel they only need to work on the relationship with their supervisors. Not so! In fact, find out which of your colleagues have relational capital with your supervisor or manager, the reason they do, and how you can develop this relational capital to advance your progress in the organisation. Just ensure it is for good reasons that can never be questioned as you advance in the organisation.

(**Identify the influencers in your department or unit and the wider company**. These are the persons who have clout (influence) with the holders of key positions such as the offices of the Chief Executive Officer (CEO), Chief Operating Officer (COO), Financial Controller (FC) or Chief Financial Officer, Chief Technology Officer (CTO), Chief Human Resource Officer (CHO) or Human Resource Director (HRD), General Manager (GM) or Managing Director (MD). Know who these key persons hold in high regard or favour and find out the reasons why they are favoured. Use those reasons to inform your progress or plans for upward mobility where they do not conflict with your personal and professional values as well as the company's values.

(**Familiarise yourself with the organisational structure as well as the departmental structure of the company**. These are organisational charts which outline the hierarchy, positions and reporting relationships of the line and management staff of the company.

CHAPTER 19

WORK ETHICS AND PROFESSIONALISM

WORK ETHICS

The Merriam-Webster Dictionary defines work ethics as *"a belief in work as a moral good: a set of values centred on the importance of doing work and reflected especially in a desire or determination to work hard."*

Work Ethics is also defined by Wikipedia as:

A belief that work and diligence have a moral benefit and an inherent ability, virtue or value to strengthen character and individual ability. It is a set of values centred on importance of work and manifested by determination or desire to work hard. Social ingrainment of this value is considered to enhance character through hard work that is respective to an individual's field of work.

You will do well to adhere to the company's Code of Ethics as described in the Employee Handbook, as failure to do so may lead to disciplinary action. Additionally, you will no doubt have your personal code of ethics which guide your conduct or deportment.

Both should always inform your decisions and positions taken when matters of ethics arise. Congruence in your beliefs or ethics and your actions is therefore critical.

PROFESSIONALISM

Let us now address a few key areas that can determine your corporate success or failure – simply put, your **professionalism**. You are described as a professional when you can exemplify the following traits in a positive manner or manage the undermentioned areas maturely:

Attitude

It is no mistake that I start with attitude. In fact, it is deliberate.

The Meriam Webster Dictionary defines attitude as "*a settled way of thinking or feeling about something.*" Also, "*truculent or uncooperative behaviour*" as attitude can be positive or negative.

My grandmother used to say that "manners maketh the man". Years later as a mature adult, I can affirm that manners indeed maketh the man and woman, the boy and the girl. I go further to say that a humble, receptive, positive and teachable spirit and attitude will make all the difference in your work life and will cause you to be promoted much more quickly than the colleague with a negative attitude, though that person may have more qualifications and experience than you have.

Take my word and experience for it!

How do you cultivate an admirable attitude?
   ☾ Start with the mind and think positive thoughts.
   ☾ Be pleasant and warm.
   ☾ Be polite and respectful of others.

- Be approachable and always have a welcoming facial expression and deliberate, positive non-verbal communication e.g. body language, posture, etc.
- Ask close friends for feedback on your aura and energy
- Always conduct introspection especially after confrontation or disagreement with others to see where you went wrong or if you were wrong.
- Read Napoleon Hill's book on *How to Win Friends and Influence People*
- Read John Maxwell's book on *"Attitude 101"*

An Excellent Spirit

Excellence is defined by the Meriam Webster Dictionary as *"the quality of being outstanding or extremely good"*.

An excellent spirit and mindset will cause you to project excellence in all you do, such as:

- Excellence in your personal presentation (e.g., your demeanour and attire)
- Excellence in your professional presentation
- Excellence in your quality of work
- Excellence in your quantity of work
- Excellence in your verbal and written communication

Attendance and Punctuality

- Be on time, all the time.
- Do not watch the clock for the departure time but leave a few minutes after the end of your official work time periodically.

- Before you depart at close of business, ask your supervisor or manager if he/she wishes you to do anything prior to leaving. This will cause you to advance quickly, as it shows you are not exact with your time, and you care about going the extra mile for the company.

- Offer to sometimes get the lunch for your manager or supervisor before you take your own lunch. You are not "kissing ass" as the expression goes but showing that you care for your supervisor or manager and are a considerate person.

- Return from personal errands as quickly as possible and if the time requested extends longer than expected, report immediately to your supervisor upon your return and let him/her know that you will work back the time that very afternoon. Now, you would certainly not claim overtime! So, be honest.

- If you are running late, you must call your supervisor or manager in advance of your work start time and advise of the time you will arrive and the reason, why you are running late. Do not forget the reason as they usually listen for that.

- Offer to work back the company's time if you requested some time to take care of other personal business like going to the bank, etc., and the time became protracted. Your manager will see that you are fair and wish to deliver an honest day's work for an honest day's wage.

Remember, it is the little things that count once you are winning in the area of your expertise. These areas and the extra "fluff" that you are willing to exemplify on the job will catapult you into your career.

Reliability and Dependability

These qualities are very high in the employer's basket of goodies and can see you being promoted very quickly. When your manager knows that he or she can leave you with a time-driven project and you deliver on time or before time, you are adding to your professional reserves. Also, when you report on time and preferably, before time, but do not seek to leave on the dot of departure time, that will increase the deposits in your good employee account (GEA).

Communication
Self:

- ❨ Strive for clear, amicable communication at all times.

- ❨ Be diplomatic especially in conversations or situations requiring much tact and sensitivity.

- ❨ Guard your non-verbal communication

With others:

- ❨ Seek to understand and ensure they understand you by listening keenly and reframing where necessary.

Email communication:

- ❨ Never reply to an email when you are upset about a matter; wait a day or two when you have calmed yourself, then reply objectively, respectfully and calmly.

- ❨ Always reply all in an email to a group of persons that requires everyone's response to be seen by the group; not just to the sender. It is disrespectful to respond only to the sender and leave the others who were copied in the dark. It also causes the communication to be incomplete.

- ❨ If the other members of the group need not be concerned or kept in the picture, indicate in the group that you will reply separately to the key person in lieu of replying to everyone in the group mail. This will ensure that persons are not kept wondering about the response or lack thereof.

- ❨ Do not use emails to avoid direct telephone or face-to-face communication; nothing is better than seeing the face of the person and hearing the voice of the person with whom you are communicating. There are also less opportunities for misunderstanding which sometimes happen with email communication and less time to correct any misunderstanding.

❨ If a matter can be resolved by directly going to the person's desk to speak with him or her or requesting a meeting rather than working out the issues in the email forum, that is highly recommended and can prevent a lot of misunderstanding plus save on valuable time.

❨ Acknowledge all emails which are directly addressed to you.

❨ Do not blind copy persons who are immaterial to the subject matter of an email and who do not need to be aware of it.

❨ Do not forward emails unnecessarily or just to share information that should not be shared or that is confidential.

Confidentiality

This is a trait that is critical and one of the quickest to become known for!

Always be confidential and ensure that no one can ever quote you in the grapevine or otherwise, unless it is for something very positive and uplifting. This trait is even more critical if you are assigned to work in the following departments, which handle very sensitive matters:

❨ Information Technology

❨ Human Resources

❨ Accounting

❨ The Corporate Office (housing the C-suite)

Assertiveness vs Aggression

Yes, there is a difference!

❦ Assertiveness is to be direct in a firm but respectful manner (my definition) whereas aggression is being overbearing and arrogant to the point where such behaviour could be repulsive and destructive to others. Know when to apply which and with whom.

❦ If you are in Sales, a mix of the right and subtle degree of aggression with strong assertiveness is usually required in order to win clients and not repel them. Some employers mistakenly think that more aggression than assertiveness is necessary for Sales but that is incorrect.

The Personal vs the Professional

Always separate the two!

Compartmentalise your personal life as much as possible and keep it distinct from your professional life.

Romantic Relationships

This should be avoided as much as possible unless you are at different locations and, even then, you need to be mindful of the company's policy which is your guide. Remember that if the relationship breaks down and your spouse is unhappy and spiteful, your intimate matters could become corporate grapevine discussions or gossip.

Avoid every relationship that could compromise your professionalism whether the relationship is vertical or horizontal, i.e. between you and your supervisor or manager; between yourself and a colleague on your level; or even between yourself and a colleague below your organisational level.

Platonic Friendships

(It is acceptable to have friends in the office; however, do ensure that if you get promoted sooner than your friends and you have to supervise them, the friendship will withstand the challenges associated with your new manager/supervisor-subordinate relationship. If this happens, them be prepared to lose some friends. If the friend's level of maturity is high, then the friendship, on the other hand, could be strengthened; however, it takes a very high level of maturity to make it work.

(Also, know that everyone will not necessarily be singing your praises; therefore, do not be disappointed once you recognise this.

The Grapevine

The grapevine is defined as the informal communication pipeline which can be true, false or distorted. Most times, it is distorted.

Be careful when quoting others from the grapevine, as this could be detrimental to your reputation if the information being quoted is inaccurate or downright wrong. However, the grapevine does serve its purpose and will make you cognizant of what others have to say about a myriad of issues pertaining to the organisation - and then some.

Dress Code

(Adhere to the Dress Code of the organisation. Every company has one.

(Do not deviate from the Code because your colleague wears something that is not approved. Your supervisor's reaction to you may not be nice, and this could impact your performance review. It also shows that you care about following the crowd than adhering to the organisation's standards.

❨ The only time you deviate is if you have a medical condition e.g., wearing a sandal because of a stubbed toe, in which case you must justify this by submitting a medical certificate requesting reasonable accommodation.

Social Media Management

No one can underrate the effectiveness of social media marketing and the impact of social media on all aspects of our lives. What is critical to observe is to refrain from sharing any comments or information about your personal life that you do not wish your employer or a prospective employer to know about you or to ask you about during an interview. A lot of persons make this mistake and never think of the implications of cyber sharing. Many recruiters actually make the decision not to call applicants for interviews based on their findings when the prospective candidates are researched on the various social media platforms.

I can recall a situation wherein a sales executive applied for a sales role and was not selected after near nude pictures of her were discovered on social media. Were it not for this poor judgement, she would have been hired for the job.

Despite the negatives of social media, Linked-In is a great business and career networking site to establish your presence as a professional.

Bad-mouthing Companies

Finally, refrain from speaking ill about the company you are working with or any company for that matter especially with regards to airing personal grouses publicly, as you may very well end up being an employee of that company in the future. Your comments may return to haunt you if a savvy recruiter, who is an excellent researcher, is able to uncover what you have shared. This can hurt your chances for great job prospects and promotional opportunities.

When your Supervisor/Manager Undermines You

❨ Do not take it personal.

❨ Let the moment pass then seek a meeting with your supervisor or manager to discuss the matter. The timing of this meeting is everything.

❨ Ensure you are not upset when you go to the meeting.

❨ During the meeting, express how you felt and ask what led to the comment.

❨ If your supervisor or manager does not admit wrongdoing, intentionally or unintentionally, indicate that you would hope it will not be repeated as it lowers your morale and is a demotivator.

❨ Thank him or her for the time to meet with you.

❨ Release all hostility and ensure you do not walk in offence, especially if you are a Christian believer.

❨ Essentially, maintain your professionalism as if nothing happened so that it cannot be used against you during your performance review.

When your Co-worker Tries to Sabotage or Undermine You

❨ Mark that person and be wary in future interactions.

❨ If you do not work directly with that person, possibly, it is not worth pursuing.

❨ If you work directly with that person, avoid heated confrontation but still address the matter one-on-one if you feel it is worth a try.

❨ Arrange your work in such a way to make it difficult, if not impossible, for that colleague to sabotage you or your work.

❨ Notify your supervisor or manager if you have concerns that it may continue.

❨ Avoid eating from that person.

❨ Avoid giving that individual access to your personal space and personal property.

❨ Avoid accommodating that person at your workstation.

Social Etiquette

The use and display of proper social graces.

Behavour at Company Events

❨ Even if the event is a social one, still maintain a professional degree of decorum. The rule of thumb is never to act in such a way that you cannot look your colleagues and management in the eyes the next day when you return to work or you have to blush when you see them. This also applies to how you dress for the company's social events.

❨ If you know you normally get drunk easily, avoid drinking.

❨ Do not show up with someone who was not invited or permitted to accompany you without first asking if you are allowed to be accompanied by a guest.

❨ Adhere to the dress code for the event.

❨ Watch your serving sizes and do not overload your plate on the first go or chase the waiter repeatedly for more drinks or food. If it is a buffet, do remember that you are allowed to help yourself more than once, so there is really no need to panic and think that the food may run out on you.

Dealing with Workplace Negativity and Conflicts

❨ Identify it and do not become a part of it otherwise you will be labelled negatively or as the mastermind behind it all. This could also hurt your chances for upward mobility/promotion.

❨ Avoid the instigators of workplace negativity and frequent conflicts as best as possible; have little to do with them.

● Avoid gossipers who usually feed the workplace negativity and contribute to workplace disharmony and confusion.

● Identify the habits that lead to a toxic and dysfunctional office environment.

● Be proactive and discuss with your supervisor or manager methods to diffuse incendiary situations that may lead to toxicity.

You have now seen that all the above constitute professionalism!

Always strive to be remembered as a true, ethical professional!

CHAPTER
20

REQUESTING A SALARY INCREASE

(Before you do, check the local salary data in your jurisdiction and sector to determine if you are already being paid at the market rate.

(If you confirm that you are already being paid at the market rate, delay requesting an increase, as you will not be able to justify the request.

(If you are below the market rate, before you request an increase, review the company's compensation philosophy to remind yourself of the process of salary reviews, timing, etc. Most companies will tell you that the granting of salary increases is based on a number of factors including affordability, value of the job, market rate, inflation, competitiveness, etc.

(Timing is everything so bear the following in mind:

❀ Choose a time when your manager or supervisor is most receptive.

✿ Choose a time when you know your performance has been consistently excellent over time and you have taken on a substantial amount of new duties and responsibilities, so there is little need for much justification of the salary increase request.

✿ Ensure that you have been with the company for at least one year and in your substantive position for at least one year.

☾ If you stand to benefit from an annual across-the-board salary increase, your justification for a separate salary increase will have to be stronger, e.g. much greater scale of responsibilities, not having received a salary increase for a long while, etc.

A Note on Building Wealth

Recognise that you will never be able to build lasting wealth using just the income from your monthly salary — your day job! No matter the number of salary increases you get and the quantum of the increases, that sole income will just not cut it!

Consequently, from early on in your career, you must start saving and investing consistently. Invest in stocks, bonds, real estate and other asset classes using sound advice from stockbrokers, wealth and financial advisors.

Capitalise on this when you are young, and you will thank me when you see the value of your investments and compound interest as you grow older.

CHAPTER
21

HOW TO GET PROMOTED QUICKLY

❨ Be an effective leader and know the difference between a leader and a manager. There are many managers but very few leaders. Simply put, managers are persons who execute the functions of management which are planning, organising, directing or leading and controlling. Many professionals can do these. They are also very positional. On the other hand, leaders are inspirational, influential, developmental and visionary while having the ability to execute the functions of management.

❨ Know how to get along very well with others. I have seen technically competent professionals over the years who could not advance beyond a certain level, as they were very poor people managers. I have also seen that their inability to manage people, sadly, led to their professional demise or them being redeployed to positions that did not involve people management directly.

❨ Get a copy of the job description of the role that you wish to be promoted to. Identify the gaps that you will have to work on to get there and make an action plan with the steps to get there. Then, work assiduously on this plan.

❨ Always meet critical deadlines.

(Always be exceptional and keep one step ahead of your boss, so when he or she asks you for a report, etc., you can show that you were already proactive by quickly producing it.

(Ask your supervisor or manager how you can assist to make his or her job easier. In short, be willing to assume more.

(Seek to request cross-training opportunities in other departments and roles than the one for which you were hired. This will increase your wholistic experience, knowledge and abilities and make you more attractive to operational roles. By request, I mean that you can volunteer to work in these other departments on weekends, during your break or lunch periods or even before or after work.

(Be an effective communicator.

(Be an effective problem solver.

(Be an innovator.

(Be collaborative.

CHAPTER
22

AVOIDING BURNOUT

No matter how excited and highly motivated you are about your job, after a while, the honeymoon period ends, and you may become worn out by the demands of the job or, simply, by your efforts to balance your personal and family life with your professional life.

To ensure that you avoid burnout, always observe the following:

- ☾ Never take on more than you can manage.
- ☾ Under promise, at times, and over deliver periodically but only if it will not exact so much from you to the point where your physical and/or mental health is negatively impacted.
- ☾ Carefully balance your personal time with your professional time.
- ☾ Personal time must be reserved for vacation, travel, relaxation, spiritual time, church time, "me" time, family time, etc.

❆ Never practice taking the company's work home. Instead, discipline yourself to work an hour or two after your official end time rather than leave work and continue working from home upon arrival. No! That is not advisable. If you must do so, it should be on rare occasions.

❆ Never try to do it all. You are not a super man or a super woman.

❆ Do not be a pleaser. A pleaser always says 'yes' and refuses to say "enough is enough" or "I cannot take this on".

❆ Learn to say no. Be willing to say "I cannot assume any more duties, as my plate is full or already overflowing". This may cause offence but say it anyway - respectfully.

❆ Ensure you are truly fulfilling your life's passion and are not in the wrong career.

CHAPTER

23

BASIC UNDERSTANDING OF ORGANISATIONAL POLITICS

You may have heard of the term "office politics" or "workplace politics" and wonder what it is all about.

Workplace politics is defined by Wikepedia as "the process and behaviour that in human interactions involves power and authority. It involves the use of power and social networking within a workplace to achieve changes that benefit the individuals within it. It is also known as organisational politics or office politics."

Usually, office politics cannot be seen but it can be felt. It is like a dark, omnipresent cloud and is sometimes seen as a 'political' imperative. It definitely helps to understand the political landscape of the company you work for.

In a Harvard Business Review article entitled *The Four Types of Organisational Politics*, writer, Michael Jarrett shared the following:

Defining politics

While we would be naive if we didn't acknowledge politics as a potentially destructive force, when deployed effectively it can help the company meet its strategic goals and live up to its values, especially during organizational change.

So what is it? Organizational politics refers to a variety of activities associated with the use of influence tactics to improve personal or organizational interests. Studies show that individuals with political skills tend to do better in gaining more personal power as well as managing stress and job demands, than their politically naive counterparts. They also have a greater impact on organizational outcomes.

Executives can view political moves as dirty and will try to distance themselves from those activities. However, what they find hard to acknowledge is that such activities can be for the welfare of the organization and its members. Thus, the first step to feeling comfortable with politics requires that executives are equipped with a reliable map of the political landscape and an understanding of the sources of political capital.

Tips for Navigating Office Politics

- ❰ Recognise it for what it is, i.e., to serve people's personal and/or professional agendas.
- ❰ It becomes more important as you move up the ranks of an organisation.
- ❰ Do not become involved in it at the expense of your output, as the political agenda could be designed to cause your downfall or failure.
- ❰ Build bridges
- ❰ Make allies
- ❰ Recognise that organisations are inherently political

- Use it to your advantage when you need to, as office politics is not all bad. Just ensure you do not compromise your values, conducts and beliefs.

- Use the various developmental and operational networks to your advantage.

- Cultivate relational capital with key movers and shakers whilst never underestimating the "undercover" or "quiet" movers and shakers with clout.

- Do trade-offs where necessary.

- Recognise that there is usually a meeting before the general meeting where key decisions are already made and which influence the wider, general meeting. This prior meeting can be held at a private dinner, a bar, an informal gathering or over breakfast or lunch.

- Be cognizant that there are certain games that you will never win, so stay away from those.

- Be sensitive to the political undercurrents.

- Understand and capitalise on organisational dynamics.

- Form alliances with the gatekeepers of the key senior executives or executive management.

- Develop your own influence and learn how to influence others.

- Recognise that your promotion may be tied to your ability to navigate office politics successfully.

- Recognise that office politics can be a dirty business but keep it clean as best as you can or as best as is within your power to do so.

CHAPTER

24

TIPS FOR KEEPING YOUR JOB

The best means of keeping your job is consistent performance and meeting or outperforming the objectives outlined in your performance management system **undergirded by a positive work attitude**.

What is the performance management system, instrument or tool?

It is the tool or framework used to measure your performance and tangible contribution to the company. It helps you and your manager or supervisor to set business and personal objectives for the appraisal year against which you may be measured either quarterly, semi-annually or annually.

Other Tips
- Ensure consistent quality of output
- Ensure consistent quantity of output
- Ensure consistency and reliability, generally, in all areas
- Consistently go the extra mile

❦ Consistently seek opportunities for cross-training or assisting in other departments different from the one in which you work or are assigned to work.

❦ Be willing to assume responsibility for special projects and/or assuming additional job responsibilities

❦ From early on, identify the influencers or the persons with clout and get on their side or get their approval in a subtle way but not if you have to compromise.

❦ For Christians, use your gift of discernment to identify the persons who operate under the spirits of Jezebel and/or Ahab. These are those who are driven by these spirits and you can research some of their characteristics and how these are displayed in the office, in the home, in personal relationships, in the church, etc.

❦ Know the issues to stay away from especially when they involve managers above your pay grade.

❦ Listen and observe more than you speak.

❦ When your spirit is uncomfortable with someone, follow your intuition and have minimal contact with that person, as the Holy Spirit may just be cautioning you about that individual.

❦ Never be too trusting or if you are, ensure, you are reposing trust in the right people.

❦ Take an extended time before you form very close relations.

Regrettably, if your relationship with your manager or supervisor is not working out and you are unable to get a transfer to another department or resolve the issues, you may have to seriously consider moving on, gracefully.

CHAPTER

25

MOVING ON GRACEFULLY

So, the job did not work out or you felt that the culture was not for you. You might have felt that your supervisor's personality was rather challenging and demotivated you rather than inspired you. The work environment was unhealthy and toxic. Indeed, there was much workplace negativity which you found offensive, leaving you no choice but to resign.

How do you move on in a professional and respectful manner?

Firstly,

a) Provide your employer with the notice period outlined in your employment contract or agreement. Do your best to honour this. If you are a line-level staff, more than likely it will be a minimum of two weeks. However, if you are a supervisor or a manager, it may be four weeks or one month. For more senior management roles, the notice period can be up to three months depending on whether the executive works in the private or the public sector. Some companies may classify you as a non-rehire if you do not give the requisite notice, which is critical for transition of your job functions to your replacement.

b) Maintain your positive and professional attitude displayed during your earlier tenure up to the point of leaving. Some employees start displaying a negative attitude because they know they are leaving. This is the worst approach you could take, as you do not wish to throw away all the relational capital and professional reputation you worked so hard to build in your last two or four remaining weeks on the job. Such negative behavour may also lead to a poor recommendation should your new employer call the company for one.

c) Maintain consistency in attendance, reliability and the observance of company policies.

d) Maintain maximum respect to your employer and your colleagues.

e) Write a decent resignation that is complimentary to the company.

f) Request at least two written references, one from your immediate supervisor and one from the supervisor's manager or the senior supervisor that you can take with you for your new employer. If you held multiple roles, one reference could be obtained from each manager or supervisor in the departments you worked.

Finally, never burn your bridges behind you even if you were disrespected by your supervisor or manager or if they were offended by your decision to leave.

CHAPTER
26

BUDGETING AND YOUR FIRST PAY CHEQUE

So, congratulations are again in order!

You have completed your first month on the job and received your first salary and your first pay slip! Brake up because if you have not received it, then ask for it.

The pay slip is a record of your earnings/income and the statutory deductions, i.e. taxes, that must be paid over to the Government of the country in which you live. It also shows the year-to-date taxes. The difference between your gross earnings and your gross expenses will leave you with your net or take-home salary. Always check the information on your pay slip to ensure accuracy.

A basic budget template that you can begin using from early in your career is shared below:

DETAILS	COST (USD)	AMOUNT/BALANCE (USD)
INCOME:		
Monthly net income		US$3,000.00
Additional income		-
TOTAL INCOME		**US$3,000.00**
MONTHLY FIXED AND SEMI-FIXED EXPENSES:		
Tithing (10%)		
Savings (10%)		
Rent or mortgage (if living on your own) OR		
Room & board (if still living with your parents)		
Property taxes		
Transportation/Petrol (if you own a car)		
Car insurance		
Education (if still studying part time while		
Supermarket/Groceries		
Telephone		
Utilities (cable, Internet, water, light, etc.)		
Life insurance		
VARIABLE EXPENSES:		
Entertainment		
Vacation		
Clothing		
Dining out		
TOTAL EXPENSES		
DEFICIT/SURPLUS		

Of course, you can customise this budget template to your needs from month to month and include your formulae in a Microsoft Excel worksheet. It will truly serve you well.

CHAPTER

27

NAVIGATING PERSONALITY TYPES

According to Dr. Kimberly Alyn, best-selling author and international professional speaker, there are four general personality types:

(Analyticals

(Amiables

(Drivers

(Expressives

Here is a summary of each category's traits:

ASK	TELL	TASK	RELATION-SHIP
Reserved	Outgoing	Guards emotions	Shares emotions
Thoughtful decisions	Quick decisions	Serious	Playful (even at work)
Avoids confrontation	Doesn't mind confrontation	Disciplined about time	Often late or forgetful
Patient	Impatient	Comfortable working alone	Prefers working with others

ASK	TELL	TASK	RELATION-SHIP
Reserves opinions	Shares Opinions	Dress: Formal	Dress: Informal
Easy going	Intense		
(Others view you as) Shy/introverted	(Others view you as) Ambitious		

To determine which personality style you are or your colleague or supervisor is, use the following table:

Ask plus Task equal…	Analytical
Ask plus Relationship equal…	Amiable
Tell plus Relationship equal…	Expressive
Tell plus Task equal…	Driver

THE TRAITS, STRENGTHS AND WEAKNESSES OF EACH PERSONALITY TYPE

ANALYTICS		
TRAITS	STRENGTHS	WEAKNESSES
Thoughtful	Perfectionist	Can be moody, critical and negative
Serious and purposeful	Neat and tidy	Can be indecisive and over-analytical
High standards of performance	Economical	
Orderly and organised		
Dry, witty sense of humour		
To manage them: Do not pressure them for decisions; have correct facts and information; give them time alone; be in ask mode; and give them encouragement when making decisions. They appreciate leaders who are careful in their decision-making and do not take costly shortcuts.		

AMIABLES		
TRAITS	**STRENGTHS**	**WEAKNESSES**
Patient	Easy going and likeable	Can be stubborn
Well balanced	Does not like conflict	Can be selfish
Quiet but witty	Diplomatic	Avoids conflict
Sympathetic	Calm	
Kind and inoffensive		

To manage them: Be gentle, do not stress them, work closely with them and be extra kind and considerate to them, as they do not do well with harsh leaders.

EXPRESSIVES		
TRAITS	**STRENGTHS**	**WEAKNESSES**
Love to have fun	Outgoing	Can be disorganised
Humorous	Ambitious	Can be undisciplined
Generous	Charismatic	Can be loud and talkative
Want to be included	Persuasive	

To manage them: Know that they are more productive if they can have fun while working; give them relationship time; show appreciation for their sense of humour and charisma. Ensure that you check their facts and give them broad structure in their jobs and the freedom to do their work. Do not give them detailed methods.

DRIVERS		
TRAITS	**STRENGTHS**	**WEAKNESSES**
Dynamic and active	Determined	Can be insensitive and un-sympathetic
Not easily discouraged	Independent and productive	Can be harsh, proud and sarcastic
Natural-born leader	Visionary	Not always detail-oriented
Confident	Decisive	Does not like to admit when wrong
Greatly dislike being micromanaged		

DRIVERS		
TRAITS	STRENGTHS	WEAKNESSES
To manage them: Get to the point and avoid too many details as they do not need all the facts to make a decision; be in task mode; give them responsibility; show appreciation for their ability to get things done; give them freedom. If you want to get to know them or speak with them, work with them on a project. Drivers appreciate leaders who will let them find the best path for reaching goals.		

Interesting information! Isn't it?

You can also use varied personality tests, instruments or psychometric tests to ascertain your personal style and behavioural tendencies as well as those of others. These instruments are usually highly scientific and give recruiters a more objective basis to make meaningful hiring decisions and increase their chances of a successful hire.

CHAPTER

28

WORKING IN A MULTI-GENERATIONAL WORKFORCE

In a multi-generational workforce, you will find the following five groups of diverse workers, which bring diversity and balance to an organisation.

It is important to know the traits and behavioural tendencies of these groups. Furthermore, knowing their communication styles can be very useful to ensure your successful interaction and collaboration with them.

1. Traditionalists

2. Baby boomers

3. Generation X

4. Generation Y – also known as Millennials

5. Generation Z

1. Traditionalists:

Traditionalists are 70 years old and above and remain in the workforce generally as partners, managers, and senior support staff. They are typically hardworking and loyal employees; however, they can be technology challenged.

2. Baby Boomers:

Baby boomers are people born between 1947 and 1965. They are also hardworking and are motivated by their position. They are dedicated and career focused as well as loyal employees. However, they, unlike traditionalists, have been exposed to technology and are quite competitive in the workplace.

3. Generation X:

Generation X are individuals born between 1966 and 1980. They are believed to be the generation that began to introduce a work/life balance. They are highly independent and self-sufficient and although they may not be as tech-savvy as the younger generations, they are quite comfortable with using technology.

4. Millennials/Generation Y:

Millennials, also known as Generation Y, are individuals born between 1981 and 1997. Like Generation X, they prefer work/life balance and flexibility. They dislike being micromanaged and prefer working from home. They would much prefer finding the most effective way to complete their work with a work smart, not hard, mantra. They thrive on innovation and have contributed significantly to the start-up mentality. They are extremely comfortable using technology and understand how to use it to their advantage.

5. Generation Z:

Generation Z comprises individuals born between 1998 and 2010. Their values and expectation differ slightly from millennials. Generally, Generation Z prefer career stability and are the most tech-savvy out of all the generations which comprise the workforce.

It is important that you learn to work with each group, as this tells your employer that you appreciate and embrace generational diversity and, of course, the cultural diversity which accompanies each group. This is very important when you have to work across cultures and especially if you work with a multi-national corporation.

CHAPTER 29

LASTING, TIME-TESTED VALUES

Finally, here are some time-tested, lasting values and attributes that will serve you well in the corporate world and help you to achieve sustained, lifetime success and favour:

- ◖ Humility
- ◖ Integrity
- ◖ Credibility
- ◖ Dependability
- ◖ Reliability
- ◖ Loyalty
- ◖ Consistency
- ◖ Excellence
- ◖ Confidence
- ◖ Trustworthiness
- ◖ Truthfulness
- ◖ Continuous learning and development
- ◖ Flexibility and versatility
- ◖ Adaptability
- ◖ Confidentiality
- ◖ Respect
- ◖ Accountability
- ◖ Good manners
- ◖ A pleasing personality

CHAPTER

30

CHARGE TO BELIEVERS

If you are a believer, please do not become a self-fulfilling prophecy to the words, often echoed, that "Christians cause the most trouble in organisations".

No way!

Please prove Corporate and the naysayers wrong! Prove your colleagues wrong too! Let them know that…:

- (You are not ordinary!
- (You bring light, newness and a unique difference to the workplace.
- (You bring the glory of God to the workplace.
- (You are exemplary!
- (You are not like your colleagues who are non-believers.
- (You operate at a much higher level as a child of God!
- (Your standards are much higher than the standards of your colleagues and the world's. Therefore, your performance will be driven by a high degree of excellence.

- ☾ Your values are much more solid and lasting than the values of your colleagues and the world's because you represent Christ and the values espoused in the bible, the Word of God!

- ☾ Your actions are always in congruence with your beliefs and values as a Christian; therefore, you have integrity and credibility. This is critical!

If you truly represent Christ, walk like it, talk like it, look like it, and be God's Ambassador to the Glory of God, your Father!

Only then will the Lord say, "Well done, thou good and faithful servant! You represented me well in the marketplace!"

Finally, do remember that your career is not your divine calling, purpose or assignment. Make the distinction and find out what your true life's purpose is according to God's blueprint for your life. He will hold you responsible for its discovery and fulfilment. No career will ever be able to replace it and give you the lasting fulfilment, joy and contentment that your divine assignment will provide.

CHAPTER
31

AFFIRMATIONS FOR THE WORLD OF WORK

I am strong.

I am assertive.

I am confident!

I am competent!

I am dependable.

I am highly trustworthy.

I am fearfully and wonderfully made! (Psalm 139:14)

I am ready to take on the marketplace as a fully equipped man or woman of God!

I add value to my role and to my organisation.

I add value to the contributions and development of others.

I value and show interest in others

I am highly favoured!

My gift makes room for me and cause me to appear before kings and great men (Proverbs 18:16).

I operate with a spirit of excellence at all times and that causes others to be drawn to me and recognise me (Daniel 6:3).

I am respected and valued by my peers.

I am respected and valued by my supervisor and my manager.

I walk in authority.

I act and operate in the role that I wish to be promoted to, not just my current role.

I am approachable.

I show that I value team work because I am a team player.

END NOTE/FINAL WORD

You have been adequately prepared for your first entry into the world of work.

Whatever was not covered in this book will be gleaned through:

- "Your pursuit of God and his resulting guidance and personal download to you on specifically how you should order the various aspects of your life. After all, Proverbs 19:21 (NIV) states *"Many are the plans in a person's heart, but it is the LORD's purpose that prevails."* Also, Psalm 37:5 (NKJV) states, *"Commit your way to the Lord, trust also in Him and He shall bring it to pass."* If you are a Christian believer, these scriptures provide you with a large part of the blueprint for your life.

- Your personal experiences

- Mentors and coaches for the specific areas of need – this is highly encouraged

- Your learning and development pursuits to hone your skills as a professional.

Through these various means, you will mature and become increasingly knowledgeable, emotionally intelligent and wise.

STEP OUT NOW WITH CONFIDENCE ON THE WORLD STAGE OF GREATNESS AND MAKE YOUR PERSONAL AND PROFESSIONAL IMPACT IN THE WORLD OF WORK!

APPENDICES

APPENDIX 1
SAMPLE JOB APPLICATION LETTER

APPENDIX 2
SAMPLE RESUME

APPENDIX 3
SAMPLE THANK YOU LETTER - POST INTERVIEW

APPENDIX 4
SAMPLE INTERVIEW QUESTIONS & ANSWERS

APPENDIX 5
SAMPLE RESIGNATION LETTER

APPENDIX 6
SAMPLE LETTER REQUESTING A SALARY REVIEW

APPENDIX 7
SAMPLE PROFESSIONAL ATTIRE IMAGES

APPENDIX 1

SAMPLE JOB APPLICATION LETTER

January ....20...

Mr. John Doe
Chief Human Resource Officer
Company ABC Ltd.
Suite #16, Maripolo Ave.
San Francisco
California, U.S.A.

Dear Mr. Doe:

RE: APPLICATION FOR THE POST OF HUMAN RESOURCES MANAGER

I am honoured to submit my application for the vacant position of Human Resources Manager with your organisation. It is encouraging and reassuring to see that I have met all the job specifications of the role, as advertised.

Kindly find enclosed my curriculum vitae which outlines the depth of my knowledge, skills and expertise for the role. With over twenty (20) years' experience in various human resource management capacities, I can add tremendous value, wisdom and diversity as an effective human resources leader and business partner in your organisation.

I look forward to receiving an invitation to be interviewed for the role of Human Resources Manager at your earliest convenience. Please contact me on any of the telephone numbers in my letterhead to arrange this.

Yours sincerely,

Cheryl Campbell
HUMAN RESOURCES MANAGER
/cc
Enc

APPENDIX 2

SAMPLE RESUME

CURRICULUM VITAE – JOHN DOE

Mailing address: P.O. Box 259, Montego Bay P.O. #1, St. James, Jamaica

Telephone: (876) 833-9999

Email: info@jamaicahrsolutions.com

CAREER OBJECTIVE

To use my knowledge, skills and expertise to add value to the organisation of which I am a team member by supporting and executing the strategic plans, mission and vision of the organisation.

MAJOR ACCOMPLISHMENTS

- Successfully prevented employees from being unionised by resolving major grievances and labour disputes.

- Successfully established a canteen, concessionaire, gymnasium and nursery for a 350-staff complement.

- Compiled and implemented, through training programmes, a comprehensive Employee Handbook with detailed company policies and a Customer Service Manual to guide the customer service division.

CAREER SPAN IN HUMAN RESOURCE MANAGEMENT

- Human Resources Director – Jamaica Development Ltd., Montego Bay, Jamaica - January 2023 to present
- Human Resources Manager – Appleton Rums Ltd., Kingston, Jamaica - January 2015 to December 2022)
- Human Resources Officer – Ford Motors Inc., U.S.A. – January 2010 to December 2014

Successful management of the following functions in the aforementioned roles:

- Total Rewards/Compensation and Benefits
- Recruitment and Termination
- Records Management
- Staff Engagement and Welfare
- Talent Management

QUALIFICATIONS

- Masters Degree in Human Resource Management – Nova Southeastern University, Florida U.S.A.
- Bachelors Degree in Business Administration - University of Technology, Jamaica

PROFESSIONAL AFFILIATIONS

- Member – Society of Human Resource Management (SHRM), Virginia, U.S.A.

REFERENCES - Available upon request

APPENDIX 3

SAMPLE THANK YOU LETTER – POST INTERVIEW

January ....20...

Mr. John Doe
Human Resources Manager
Company ABC Ltd.
10 Belmont Road
Kingston

Dear Mr. Doe:

I wish to express my gratitude to you for granting me an interview on Monday, January..., 20... for the role of Administrative Manager. It was truly a pleasure meeting with you and your team to share my strengths and the value I can bring to your organisation.

I wish to reiterate that I am a fully qualified Administrative Manager who meets all the expectations that you require of the role, as advertised, and as shared during our interview session. Not only can I deliver on the objectives attached to the role but I can also bring additional knowledge, skills and abilities to impact the organisation meaningfully.

I look forward to receiving an offer of employment to commence working with your company as early as Monday, January...20... I can guarantee that you will realise a significant return on your investment in me.

Yours sincerely,

Cheryl Campbell

APPENDIX 4

SAMPLE INTERVIEW QUESTIONS & ANSWERS

Below are some frequently asked questions by interviewers or recruiters, which are frequently not answered correctly or substantially. The suggested answers should better position you to ace the job! Note, also, that there are many effective videos that can be accessed on Internet sites, such as YouTube, with valuable questions and answers for all types of positions in many of the popular job classifications. You will do well to research these.

NUM	QUESTION	SUGGESTED ANSWERS
1	Tell me about your weaknesses	**If you are a supervisor or manager:** ❮ Naturally, we all have weaknesses. I think mine would be having excessively high expectations of my staff just like I do for myself when, in reality, it does not work that way. ❮ I also get impatient when employees do not meet their deadlines, as that frustrates my efforts to meet other related deadlines. ❮ I am very disapproving of mediocrity and poor excuses for not meeting company expectations due to the high level of excellence that I place on my quality of work, quantity of work and deliverables. Therefore, in giving that feedback to subordinates, I need to convey it with more diplomacy and tact, so they do not get discouraged or demotivated. **If you are a line staff:** ❮ Naturally, we all have weaknesses. I think mine would be setting expectations of myself that are too high and, at times, unrealistic and not learning to say no when too much is on my plate.

NUM	QUESTION	SUGGESTED ANSWERS
2	Describe your strengths	**A manager's or supervisor's response**: ❰ I am more of a strategic than tactical business partner. ❰ I coach and mentor employees effectively. ❰ I quickly gain the trust, confidence and respect of my subordinates. ❰ My affable personality and authenticity. **A line staff's response**: ❰ My great interpersonal skills which make me readily able to function as a team player. ❰ My singular focus when I need to meet deadlines thereby almost always delivering well in advance of those deadlines. ❰ My persistence in working towards my goals and objectives thus resisting procrastination.
3	Tell me about yourself	❰ A doer and an influencer, I am a well-respected individual and professional in my area of expertise. Individuals and companies find me trustworthy and hail my credibility, as I act with integrity at all times and maintain consistency in how I order my life generally. ❰ I also build rapport with others quickly and easily.
4	Why are you applying for this role?	*(Describe the value of the role as advertised in relation to your need for upward mobility.)* ❰ The role seems like one that would afford me the long-awaited opportunity for upward mobility, growth and development. ❰ I am also confident that given my expert knowledge and proven experience in the field, I can bring exceptional and unique value to the manner in which the role is executed and surpass your expectations.

NUM	QUESTION	SUGGESTED ANSWERS
5	Why should we hire you?	(*Describe the value that you can bring to the company based on the hard and soft skills that are required, e.g.*) **From one with experience:** ❨ You should hire me because of my expert knowledge, proven experience and success in the field. I am well-known in the marketplace as an authority in my field and can bring exceptional and unique value to the manner in which the role is executed and ultimately, the bottom line and reputation of the company. **As a new entrant in the world of work:** ❨ You should hire me because of my strong soft skills that are necessary pre-requisites for the role of ......,. Some of these soft skills are my positive work attitude, impressive professionalism and the spirit of excellence which drives my performance generally in all aspects of my personal and professional life. ❨ Coupled with my academic qualifications, strong interest in your company and my profound intrinsic and extrinsic motivation, I am ready to make a significant impact in the quantity and quality of output as well as the innovation and creativity that your organisation expects of its team members.

Here are some great questions that you can always ask regardless of the position for which you are interviewing:

NUM	QUESTION
1	Why is this position vacant and what can I do to make a significant difference in the role?
2	How would you describe the culture of your organisation and do you agree that the senior leadership always sets the tone for the cultural direction of the company?

NUM	QUESTION
3	Please describe the path for career growth in your organisation and the support given to employees to move along that continuum to achieve upward mobility.
4	What type of leadership style is encouraged in your organisation and what do you do to encourage and maintain your selected style?
5	What are the top three challenges that you frequently contend with in your company and what strategies do you deploy to resolve them?
7	How financially stable is the company and what are some of the strategies deployed to ensure continued financial viability?
8	Please tell me about your strategic plan for the next five to ten years.
9	What is the company's compensation philosophy?
10	Have I said anything in this interview or given you any reasons to doubt that I am a good fit for the role? If so, what is that?" Also, "What else could I share with you that could assist you in your selection of me for the role?"

APPENDIX 5

SAMPLE RESIGNATION LETTER

January 1, 20…

Mr. John Brown
Managing Director
Company ABC Ltd.
10 Belford Rd
Palm Bay
Florida…..
U.S.A.

Dear Mr. Brown:

RE: RESIGNATION

It has been a pleasure to have served your organisation for the past three years in the capacity of Senior Secretary. The experience has been a most rewarding and invaluable one especially as it afforded me the opportunity to work in two departments within the company.

It is therefore with great regret that I tender my resignation from the company effective January 30, 20…, as I leave to assume a new role that will advance my career interests and upward mobility.

I wish the company continued growth and success as a market leader in the industry.

Yours sincerely,

Mary-Jane Doe

APPENDIX 6

SAMPLE LETTER REQUESTING A SALARY REVIEW

Dear Mr/Ms…..:

I wish to take this opportunity to express my appreciation for your trust and confidence in conferring me with the opportunity to work in my current role as …..

As you know, I have been in this role for the past two years, and it has been a most exciting and rewarding journey in terms of my self-actualisation, self-confidence and self-esteem. My knowledge, skills and abilities have also been enlarged and enriched. In fact, the role has expanded to the point where I have been assuming greater levels of responsibility and decision making. It is therefore against this background that I am seeking a revision of my base salary to more accurately reflect the current market rate of $x per annum.

I have observed that a few companies are paying base salaries in the range of $x to $x for the role that I currently occupy. Please refer to the attached excerpt from the ……….Salary Survey which supports the foregoing statement. (*At this point you can quote the main salary reference or body of data which outlines the most recent salary survey, the positions surveyed and the findings in respect of base salaries, allowances, incentives and other non-cash benefits*). In light of this discovery, it means that I fall below the market rate by X percentage or $x.

Would you kindly advise me of a mutually convenient time when we can meet to discuss this matter? I am readily available and look forward to our positive and favourable discussions.

Sincerely,

Mary-Jane Williams
Marketing Officer

APPENDIX 7

SAMPLE PROFESSIONAL ATTIRE IMAGES

EXECUTIVE WEAR - WOMEN

EXECUTIVE WEAR – MEN

BIBLIOGRAPHY

a) Crestcom International LLC, Greenwood Village (Suburban Denver), Colorado, U.S.A., www.crestcomleadership.com – Dr. Kim Alyn, Presenter on Techniques for Managing Personality Styles in the Bullet Proof Manager Leadership Programme.

b) Employee Connect at www.employeeconnect.com for the article, Generational Diversity in the Workplace 2022

c) https://resources.owllabs.com/blog/management-styles

d) www.metlife.com - 20th Annual US Employee Benefits Trends Study

e) The Holy Bible - King James Version (KJV), New International Version (NIV) and New King James Version (NKJV)

f) Work ethics Definition & Meaning - Merriam-Webster – www.merriam-webster.com/dictionary/work&20ethic

g) merriam-webster dictionary on attitude definition - Search (bing.com)

h) merriam-webster dictionary on excellence definition - Search (bing.com)

i) Workplace politics definition and Workplace Ethics - Wikipedia

j) Harvard Business Review - article entitled *The Four Types of Organisational Politics* - Michael Jarrett, Writer.

k) **SAMPLE PROFESSIONAL WEAR IMAGES**:
   a) **Part one title page image link**
   https://www.pexels.com/photo/woman-in-dress-sitting-in-front-of-a-laptop-10375901/

   b) **Part two title page image link**
   https://images.pexels.com/photos/6986456/pexels-photo-6986456.jpeg

c) Part three title page image link

https://images.pexels.com/photos/4651186/pexels-photo-4651186.jpeg?auto=compress&cs=tinysrgb&w=600

d) APPENDIX

EXECUTIVE WEAR – WOMEN

https://www.pexels.com/photo/a-woman-in-white-long-sleeves-holding-a-striped-blazer-12872784/

https://www.pexels.com/photo/woman-smiling-and-holding-teal-book-1181424/

https://images.pexels.com/photos/2381069/pexels-photo-2381069.jpeg?auto=compress&cs=tinysrgb&w=175&fit=crop&h=275&dpr=1

https://www.pexels.com/photo/women-in-black-blazer-standing-back-to-back-7959793/

https://images.pexels.com/photos/8069386/pexels-photo-8069386.jpeg?auto=compress&cs=tinysrgb&w=1260&h=750&dpr=1

https://images.pexels.com/photos/7651578/pexels-photo-7651578.jpeg?auto=compress&cs=tinysrgb&w=1260&h=750&dpr=1

e) EXECUTIVE WEAR – MEN

https://images.pexels.com/photos/1450114/pexels-photo-1450114.jpeg?auto=compress&cs=tinysrgb&w=1260&h=750&dpr=1

https://images.pexels.com/photos/1661416/pexels-photo-1661416.jpeg?auto=compress&cs=tinysrgb&w=1260&h=750&dpr=1

https://images.pexels.com/photos/2955376/pexels-photo-2955376.jpeg?auto=compress&cs=tinysrgb&w=1260&h=750&dpr=1

NOTES

NOTES

ANOTHER EXCITING TITLE

BY CHERYL CAMPBELL

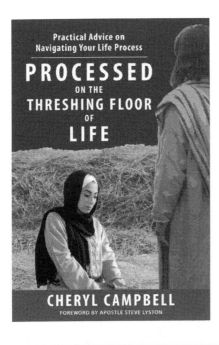

PROCESSED ON THE THRESHING FLOOR OF LIFE

Practical Advice on Navigating your Life Process

Faith, Sickness, Rejection, Poor Choices, Accidents and Near Misses...the "process of life" never ends. Once you read this amazing book and apply the invaluable Process Toolkit Strategies, you can be assured that you will view the processes of life differently.

Made in the USA
Columbia, SC
13 June 2023

17732884R10067